Imam Muhammad Shirazi

THE QUR'AN
When was it compiled?

Translated by
Ali ibn Adam

fountain books

BM Box 8545
London WC1N 3XX
UK
www.fountainbooks.co.uk

In association with
Tahrike Tarsile Qur'an, Inc.
P.O. Box 731115
Elmhurst, New York 11373
USA
www.koranusa.org

First published 2001

© *fountain books*

British Library Cataloguing in Publication Data.

A catalogue record for this book is available from the British Library.

ISBN   1-903323-05-3

Cover design by Ali Saleh

In the Name of Allah, The Beneficent The Merciful.
All Praise is to Him, Lord of the Worlds.
Let Allah's Blessings be upon Muhammad
and upon his righteous and pure family.

Table of Content

Publisher's Foreword

{Verily this Qur'an guides to that which is most upright.} [1]

The Holy Qur'an is the eternal celestial message revealed by Allah to His prophet Muhammad (Blessings and Peace be upon him and his family) so that he might rescue a confused humanity from the darkness of doubt and ignorance to the light of certainty and knowledge, for the Qur'an delineates the road of guidance and righteousness in both religious and worldly affairs.

The Qur'an represents the foundation stone of Islam, which Allah has promised to keep free from corruption:

{We have sent down the Reminder and We shall be its protectors.} [2]

Therefore the hand of corruption has not touched it like it has the other divine books. The Qur'an remains the eternal divine message that has come for humanity in its entirety. The enemies of Islam despite their efforts to the contrary, have not been able to fault the integrity of the Holy Qur'an after the challenge posed by Allah for them to bring forth even one chapter of its ilk. Human intellect has not been able to meet this challenge.

Allah Almighty says in the Qur'an:

{If you are in doubt as to that which We have sent down upon Our servant, then bring forward a chapter of its ilk and call upon your witnesses other than Allah if you speak the truth.} [3]

One of the most important reasons for the preservation of the Qur'an in addition to it being the will of Allah is the fact that the Messenger of Allah concerned himself with collating the Qur'an during his life and insisted upon it. Hence, from then until now, the Qur'an has remained the same without any change.

---

[1] *The Qur'an*: The Night Journey (17):9.
[2] *The Qur'an*: Al-Hijr (15):9.
[3] *The Qur'an*: The Heifer (2):23.

This book, *'When was the Qur'an Compiled'* by the esteemed writer and source of religious knowledge Imam Muhammad Shirazi, deals with the subject of the collation of the Qur'an. It provides firm evidence that the Holy Qur'an was compiled at the time of and at the command of the Prophet, peace be upon him, in the form in which it exists today dispelling the view of those who imagine that the Qur'an was compiled after the time of the Messenger of Allah.

The writer also tackles the question of the non-corruption of the Qur'an, which Shi'a scholars have stated throughout history refuting the notion that there has been any addition to or subtraction from the verses of the Qur'an. Imam al-Shirazi then touches upon the inauthenticity of the different 'readings' except that which is present in the holy text itself.

Finally he presents a number of traditions regarding many aspects of the Holy Qur'an. This is seen as further evidence that the Holy Qur'an was compiled in the form we have it today, and 'in use' by the Muslims during the lifetime of the holy Prophet of Islam, Muhammad peace be upon him and his infallible descendants.

Note: when a verse from the holy Qur'an is quoted, the name of the chapter in which it appears is given followed by the sequential number of the chapter and that of the verse. For example if we have The Holy Qur'an, The Resurrection (75): 17, this refers to verse number 17 of chapter 75 which is entitled Resurrection.

Publisher

February 2001

Author's Introduction

Here are a number of traditions to be found in the *'Shi'a Guide to the Shari'a'*[4] and other books regarding the importance of the Qur'an and its etiquettes and disciplines which we have mentioned hoping to bring benefit to many. We have preceded this with information about the collation of the Qur'an and its textual non-corruption and that not one word or letter has been added nor subtracted. It is the same Qur'an today that was sent down to the Messenger of Allah and was compiled by him in the same structure of verses and chapters at the command of Allah during his life.

---

[4] The Arabic title of the book is
"Tafseel Wassa'el al-Shi'a ila Tahseel Massa'el al-Shari'ah"

Part One

On the Compilation of the Holy Qur'an

The Hadith of Ibn 'Abbas

In '*al-Manaqib*' it is related that Ibn 'Abbas said: '*When Allah's words:* {**You are mortal and they are mortals.**} [5] *were revealed, Allah's Messenger (S)*[6] *said: 'If only I knew when this (my death) would be.'* This, when the Prophet (S) knew 'the unseen' with the permission and inspiration of Allah. *Then the 110ᵗʰ chapter of the Qur'an named al-Nasr (Succour) was revealed, after which the Prophet (S) remained silent between the 'takbir'[7] and the 'reading' then he used to say: 'Praise be to Allah, I seek the forgiveness of Allah and turn towards Him in repentance.'* He was asked about this and said: 'It is that my soul has foretold me of my impending death.' Then he began to weep intensely. He was then asked: 'Oh Messenger of Allah, do you weep over death when Allah has forgiven all your sins both past and future?*[8] The Prophet (S) said: 'But what of the terror of the questioning and what of the confines of the grave and the darkness of the tomb, and the resurrection and the other fearsome things?'* (Here the Prophet means to draw attention to these fearsome

---

[5] *The Qur'an*: The Groups (39):30.

[6] *Sall-Allah Alayhi wa Alihi wa Sallam,* meaning Peace and Blessings of Allah be upon him and his infallible family. This is always stated after the mention of the name of the Prophet out of respect for the Prophet of Islam (s).

[7] The takbir or takbir al-ihram (sanctification) consists of the words 'Allahu Akbar', (God is Great) which are said at the beginning of every one of the daily canonical prayers and other supererogatory prayers denoting the beginning of the prayer and the fact that the person praying has entered the sanctity of prayer. The reading mentioned here is the reading of the opening chapter of the Qur'an, which forms the basis of prayers in Islam.

[8] This is a reference to 48:2. In all cases when Allah addresses His Messenger in this way, it is meant to indirectly address the people at large to take heed. This is meant for them to take notice.

things rather than say that he will be tried by them as is clear.) *Then Ibn 'Abbas said: 'The Prophet (S) lived for a further year after the revelation of this chapter.'*[9]

Thenceforth, verse after verse was revealed until only seven days remained of the Prophet's life. Then the following verse was revealed:

{And fear ye a day in which you will be returned to Allah and every soul will be given what it has earned and they will not be dealt with unjustly.}[10]

This verse – according to certain transmissions – was the last verse of the Holy Qur'an to be revealed to the Messenger of Allah by the Archangel Gabriel who said to him:

'Place this verse at the head of the 280th verse of the second chapter.'[11]

The first verse revealed to the Prophet Muhammad (S) by the Archangel Gabriel was Allah's words: **{In the Name of Allah The Beneficent The Merciful, Read! In the name of your Lord Who has created . . .}**[12]

The first verse of the Qur'an to be revealed coincided with the first day of the noble prophetic mission and the last verse of the Qur'an to be revealed took place during the last days of the Messenger of Allah. The time between these two verses was when the rest of the Qur'an was revealed and this was over a period of 23 years.

---

[9] See *Seas of Lights*: vol.22, p.471; and also al-Manaqib: vol.1, p.234, The section on the death of the prophet (S): *Related from Ibn 'Abbas, and al-Sudayy that when Allah's words were revealed: {You are mortal and they are mortals.}, the Messenger of Allah said: 'If only I knew when this would be.', then the 110th chapter of The Qur'an named al-Nasr (Succour) was revealed and he used to remain silent during the prayer between saying 'Allahu Akbar' and the reading but he said: 'Praise be to Allah, I ask Allah for forgiveness and turn towards Him in repentance.' He was asked about this and he said: 'It is that my soul has foretold me of my impending death.' Then he began to weep intensely. They said to him: 'O Messenger of Allah, do you weep over death when Allah has forgiven your sins both past and future?' He said: 'But what of the terror of the questioning, or the confines of the grave and the darkness of the tomb, and what of the resurrection and the fearsome things!' He lived after the revelation of this chapter for a further year.*

[10] *The Qur'an*: The Heifer (2):280.

[11] *The Tafsir of al-Shubbar*: p.83, The Heifer (2).

[12] *The Qur'an*: The Clot (96):1.

Who Compiled the Qur'an?

In the previous *hadith*, what draw our attention are the words of the Archangel Gabriel to the Prophet at the time of the revelation of the final Qur'anic verse:

'*Place them at the head of the 280ᵗʰ verse of the second chapter.*'

It is then clear that Allah (through the Angel Gabriel) commanded the Prophet (S) to compile the Qur'an and to organise its structure in a precise manner even as far as the numbering of the verses. This the Prophet indeed did during his life as Allah had ordered and it was not for the Prophet (S) to leave the Qur'an disparate so that someone after him should compile it.

It is not possible that the Prophet (S) with his great concern and endeavour in preserving the Qur'an should neglect the task of compiling and structuring it and leave the Qur'an scattered amongst the Muslims and delegate the task of compiling it to them. This especially so after revelation had informed him: {**You are mortal and they are mortals.**}[13]

It is not possible that the Prophet (S) could be deeply concerned with the Qur'an on the one hand so that he would order that it should be memorised and paid attention to, and encourage its recital and the practice of its tenets particularly in his final days. He would say repeatedly:

'*I leave behind me two momentous things - the book of Allah and my kin, the people of my household. As long as you adhere to them both you will never go astray after me ever.*'[14]

It is not right that he would do this and at the same time fail to compile the Qur'an and by doing so leave it scattered.

---

[13] *The Qur'an*: The Groups (39):30.

[14] *Fiqh al-Qur'an*: vol.1,p.63, the words 'after me ever' are omitted. See also Irshad al-Qulub: p.340, '*I leave with you the two momentous things, as long as you adhere to them you will never go astray - the book of Allah and my kin the people of my household. These are the two Caliphs for you and they will never separate from one another until we meet at the well of Kauthar.*'

The Qur'an is the eternal constitution of Islam and its inimitable miracle surviving throughout the aeons and ages until the day of resurrection. It is not therefore logical to assume that the Prophet would leave the Qur'an scattered, without compiling it.

How is it conceivable that Allah should permit His Prophet (S) not to compile that Qur'an despite having said in the Qur'an: {**It is our duty to compile it and recite it.**}[15]

Allah also says: {**We have sent down the Reminder and We shall be its protectors.**}[16]

It is therefore the duty of the Prophet (S) to deliver the Qur'an as a structured whole to all people as compiled and structured by Allah.

---

[15] *The Qur'an*: The Resurrection (75): 17.
[16] *The Qur'an*: Al-Hijr (15): 9.

The Prophet Compiled the Qur'an

Therefore, the Qur'an that we have possession of today with all its structure and compilation, the numbering of its verses, and the structure of its chapters and sections is the very same Qur'an that the Prophet Muhammad (S) gathered, collated, compiled and structured for Muslims during his life at the instigation of Allah. It has not been subject to any change or corruption, substitution or modification, addition or subtraction.

Support for this comes from a report in the exegesis of 'Ali Ibn Ibrahim[17] from Imam al-Saadiq (a)[18] that the Messenger of Allah (S) ordered 'Ali ibn Abi Talib (a) to collect the Qur'an saying:

'Oh 'Ali. The Qur'an is behind my bed, in scrolls, silk and papers. Take it and collate it and do not lose it as the Jews have lost the Torah.' Thereupon Imam 'Ali (a) took it and gathered it in a yellow garment and sealed it up.[19]

This report indicates that the Prophet (S) ordered that the Qur'an be collected and that Imam 'Ali (a) was the one who collected it on the direct orders of the Prophet (S) during his lifetime.

Similarly, all Shi'a jurists agree on this point. In the Qur'anic exegesis *Majma' al-Bayan,* al-Sayyid al-Murtada is quoted as saying that the Qur'an was compiled during the lifetime of the Messenger of Allah (S) in the form that we are in possession of today. The evidence for this is that the Qur'an was studied and learnt by heart at that time as a whole so that a group of companions were chosen to memorise it. It was also shown to the Prophet (S) and recited in front of him. A group of the companions like 'Abdullah ibn Mas'oud and Ubayy ibn Ka'b and others recited the Qur'an from beginning to end in front of the Prophet (S) a number of times all of which indicates that it was in a gathered and structured form and not disparate and scattered. The same was said by Sheikh al-Mufid, Sheikh al-Sadouq and other Shi'a

---

[17] *Tafsir al-Qumi:* vol.2, p.451, The People (114).
[18] *Alayh-es-Salam* meaning peace be upon him. This is always stated after the mention of the name of one the infallible Imams out of respect for the Imam (a).
[19] *Seas of Lights:* vol.89, p.48, Beirut edition.

scholars before the time of al-Murtada, and others after him like al-Tusi and the great Qur'anic exegete al-Tabari who died in 548 A.H. as well as all of our other great scholars up to the present day.

Zaid ibn Thabit is reported as having said: '*We used to collect the fragments of the verses of the Qur'an and put them in their appropriate places at the instruction of the Messenger of Allah (S). Despite this, the verses were still fragmented so the Prophet (S) ordered 'Ali (a) to gather them in one place and warned us against losing them.*'

It is reported that al-Sha'bi said: '*The Qur'an was collected during the time of the Prophet of Allah (S) by six men of the Ansar.*'

In the book *al-Sirat al-Mustaqim*, Anas says: '*Four men collected the Qur'an during the life of the Prophet (S) those being my father, Mu'adh, Zaid (Ibn Thabit), and Abu Zaid.*'[20]

Qatada is reported as having said: '*I asked Anas about who compiled the Qur'an during the lifetime of the prophet (S). He said Four men of the Ansar, then mentioned their names.*'

Also related from Anas: '*The Prophet (S) died, four men having collected the Qur'an: Abu Darda', Mu'adh ibn Jabal, Zaid ibn Thabit, and Abu Zaid.*'[21]

Finally from 'Ali ibn Ribah: '*Ali ibn Abi Talib (a) collected the Qur'an along with Ubayy ibn Ka'b during the lifetime of the Prophet (S).*'

---

[20] *Al-Sirat al-Mustaqim*: vol.3, p.38.
[21] *Seas of Lights*: vol.92, p.77.

Other Evidence

There are other evidences which point to the fact that the Qur'an we have today is the very same as was gathered and structured during the time of the Messenger of Allah, with no additions or subtractions:

1. The 'Opening' Chapter

The naming of the first chapter of the Qur'an as the 'opening' chapter during the time of the Prophet means that it is the opening chapter of the Qur'an despite the fact that neither this chapter or even the first verse of it were the first chronologically to be revealed to the Prophet Muhammad. The naming of it as the 'opening' chapter during the Prophet's lifetime shows that the book was collated together as a whole in the form existent today, and that the first chapter then is still the first chapter today.

2. The Hadith of the "Two Momentous Things"

The Prophet (S) used to say in this *hadith* that is widely related by both Sunnite and Shi'a scholars:

'I leave with you the two momentous things – the book of Allah and the people of my household. As long as you adhere to these two you will never go astray after me.' [22]

The book that the Prophet (S) left behind for his community is the gathered and structured whole and not scattered verses otherwise the name 'book' would not be ascribed to it. [23]

---

[22] See *Seas of Lights*: vol.13, p.147: *'I leave with you the two momentous things – the book of Allah and my kin the people of my household. They will never separate until they arrive at the well (of Kauthar).'*

[23] In the lexicon *Lisan al-'Arab*, under kataba, the word kitab (book) is a noun used for what is written as a gathered whole. In the dictionary *al-Munjid*, under kataba, the word kitab (book) is something in which there is writing. It is called this because in it chapters, sections and issues are gathered.

Allah precedes his Prophet in this regard by referring to the Qur'an again and again and in numerous verses as 'The Book', alluding to the fact that it is gathered and collated with Him on the preserved tablet – as certain commentators have stated, and that He showed the Prophet its compilation and structure and ordered him to compile and structure the Qur'an as it is compiled and structured in the preserved tablet, which the Prophet duly did.

Allah speaks in the Qur'an saying: {**This is a blessed book which We have sent down, confirming (the revelation) before it, and to warn the mother of all cities and those around her, and those who believe in the hereafter will believe in it while they are steadfast in their prayers.**}[24]

He, Almighty is He, also says: {**He has the keys to the unseen, none know of them save He and He knows what is in the land and in the sea, not a leaf drops but that He is aware of it nor a seed in the darkness of the earth, nor anything wet or dry but that it is in a clear book.**}[25]

He Almighty is He also says: {**O people of the book, Our messenger has come to you to make plain to you much of that which you have been concealing of the book and to forgive much. From Allah has come to you a light and an elucidating book.**}[26]

And He Almighty is He has said: {**And this is a blessed book which We have sent down so follow ye it and adopt piety so may ye be shown mercy.**}[27]

And He Almighty is He has said: {**A book sent down to you so let there be no shame in your breast to warn with it and as a reminder to those who have faith.**}[28]

And He Blessed is He has said: {**A book whose verses have been made firm and then explained from the auspices of the wise the knowing.**}[29]

---

[24] *The Qur'an*: The Livestock (6): 92.
[25] *The Qur'an*: The Livestock (6): 59.
[26] *The Qur'an*: The Table Spread (5): 15.
[27] *The Qur'an*: The Livestock (6): 155.
[28] *The Qur'an*: The Heights (7): 2.
[29] *The Qur'an*: The Prophet Hud (11): 1.

And He The Almighty has said: {**A book which We have sent down to you so you may bring the people out of the darkness and into the light by the permission of their Lord to the way of The All Mighty The All Praised.**}[30]

3. The Complete Recitation of the Qur'an

It is related that the Prophet (S) ordered that the Qur'an should be recited in its entirety during the month of Ramadan and at other times, and he made known the virtue and reward to be gained from its recitation. This complete recitation would have no meaning if the Qur'an had not been present as a complete structured whole as the meaning of a complete recitation (*khatm*) is to begin at the beginning of a book and to end at the end of it.[31]

The Prophet (S) said: '*Whoever completes a recitation of the Qur'an, it is as if he has reached the station of prophethood except that he does not receive revelation.*'[32]

The Prophet (S) also said: '*When the believer reads the Qur'an, Allah looks upon him with mercy and for each verse gives him one-thousand Houris and for each letter gives him a light on the path. When he completes a recitation of the Qur'an, Allah rewards him with the reward of three-hundred and thirteen prophets who carried out the message of their Lord, and it is as if he has read every book that Allah has sent down upon His prophets, and Allah forbids his body from the fire and forgives him and his parents their sins.*'[33]

'Abdullah Ibn Mas'oud and Ubayy Ibn Ka'b and others completed recitations of the Qur'an in front of the Prophet (S) a number of times. If the Qur'an had not been gathered together during his lifetime then this would not have been possible.

In the book *Mutashabih al-Qur'an*, the author says: *It is proven that the Prophet (S) read the Qur'an, compiled it and ordered that it be*

---

[30] *The Qur'an*: The Prophet Abraham (14): 1.
[31] In the lexicon *Lisan al-'Arab*, under the word khatam, a person khatama the Qur'an if he reads it to the end. In the dictionary *Al-Wasit*, khatama means to complete something and reach the end and finish with it, and it is said 'finish the Qur'an.' In the dictionary *al-Munjid*, it means to read the entire Qur'an.
[32] *Usul al-Kafi*: vol.2, p.604.
[33] *Seas of Lights*: vol.89, p.17.

11

written down in this form. Every year he would read it for the Angel Gabriel (a) once except the year of his death when he read it for him twice. A group of the companions recited it in its entirety in front of the Prophet among them Ubayy Ibn Ka'b. 'Abdullah Ibn Mas'oud recited it ten times in front of the Prophet.[34]

In the book *Seas of Lights*, the great scholar al-Majlisi says: '*Al-Bukhari, Muslim, and al-Tirmidhi in their authenticated collections of hadith relate from Anas: 'The Qur'an was collected during the lifetime of the Prophet by four men of the Ansar: Ubayy Ibn Ka'b, Mu'adh Ibn Jabal, Abu Zaid, and Zaid Ibn Thabit.*[35]

4. Between the Mihrab and the Pulpit

It is also reported that the entire Qur'an was placed in a written form between the *mihrab* and the pulpit (*minbar*) and that Muslims used to copy from it.

5. Presentation of Qur'an to the Messenger of Allah

It is related that Gabriel (a) used to present the Qur'an to the Prophet (S) once every year, and in the last year of the Prophet's life he presented it to him twice. This would not have been possible had the Qur'an not been already gathered and collated.

The *hadith* report that when the Prophet (S) began to feel the effects of the illness, which afflicted him at the end of his life, he took the hand of 'Ali (a) and said: '*The trials have descended like the darkness of night. Gabriel (a) used to present (the Qur'an) to me once every year but this year he presented (the Qur'an) to me twice. It seems to me that my time is near.*'[36]

---

[34] *Mutashabih al-Qur'an*: vol.2, p.77.

[35] *Seas of Lights*: vol.89, p.77.

[36] *Qasas al-Anbiya'* of al-Rawandi: p.357, section 13.

The Prophet (S) also said: *'Gabriel (a) used to present to me the Qur'an once per year but this year he presented it to me twice. I believe that my time is near.'* [37]

6. The Memorisation of the Qur'an

It is related that a group of the Companions of the Prophet (S) had memorised the entire Qur'an by heart during the time of the Prophet (S).[38] This is clear to anyone who refers to the commentary on the Qur'an by al-Balaghi. Also in one of the issues of the periodical 'Answers to Religious Questions'[39] there is an article by (the author's father) al-Sayyid Mirza Mahdi al-Shirazi published in the holy city of Karbala.

7. Concordance with the Book of Allah

Another fact which shows that the Holy Qur'an we have today is the same Qur'an revealed to the Messenger of Allah (S) without literary corruption, or addition or subtraction are the traditions which order that any *hadith* related from the Messenger of Allah (S) or his household should be compared with the Holy Qur'an in order that the wheat be separated from the chaff. These traditions say: *'All (hadith) that is in concordance with the Book of Allah was said by the Messenger of Allah or his household. Anything that goes against the book of Allah is vain and false and was not said by them.*

These traditions refer us to the Qur'an which we have with us today in order to tell the truth from the falsehood, which points to it being free from any addition or subtraction, substitution or corruption, as a corrupted book is not fit to be the source of knowledge of the true from the false.

Related from Imam Ja'far al-Saadiq (a) is that the Prophet (S) said: *'For every truth there is a reality and for every correct practice there is a guiding light, so whatever is in concord with the book of Allah*

---

[37] *Seas of Lights*: vol.22, p.466 and vol.22, p.471.

[38] In *Seas of Lights*: vol.41, p.147: *'All are agreed upon the fact that Amir al-Mu'minin 'Ali b. Abi Talib (a) had memorised the Qur'an during the time of the Prophet (S)*

[39] This is a religious publication, which was printed in Karbala at the instigation of al-Imam al-Shirazi and was overseen by some of the most esteemed scholars.

then go by it and whatever contradicts the book of Allah then leave
it."[40]

Related also from the Purified Imams

(a). *'If you come across a hadith related from us then compare it with
the book of Allah. Whatever is in agreement with the book of Allah
then take it and whatever contradicts the book of Allah then reject it
or refer it to us.'* [41]

(b). *'If you come across two hadiths related from us then compare
them with the book of Allah, what is in concord then take it and what
is in disagreement then reject it.'* [42]

(c). *'Whatever comes to you related from us then compare it with the
book of Allah, whatever is in concord with it then accept it and what
contradicts it then reject it.'* [43]

Furthermore, there are numerous Qur'anic verses and traditions which
point out that the Qur'an was sent down upon the Messenger of Allah
(S) in two ways: once it was sent down in its entirety upon the heart
of the Messenger of Allah (S) as in the Qur'anic verse: {**Verily we
sent down revelation on the night of Qadr.**}[44], and once more in
instalments over the space of twenty-three years according to the
appropriate occasions and issues. The Prophet's heart contained the
Qur'an, which was revealed to him firstly in its entirety, then he
collated and structured the Qur'an that was revealed to him secondly
bit by bit according to the structure of the first revelation of the
Qur'an. This is the very same Qur'an as that which exists with us
today.

This and other evidence shows that the Qur'an we have today is the
Qur'an that was gathered and collated at the command of Allah and
His Messenger (S) during his lifetime without the addition or
subtraction of a single letter, or any change or substitution. For Allah

---

[40] *Usul al-Kafi*: vol.1, p.69.
[41] *Al-Tahdhib*: vol.7, p.274.
[42] *Al-Istibsar*: vol.1, p.190.
[43] *Al-Istibsar*: vol.3, p.157.
[44] *The Qur'an*: The Decree (97): 1.

has said: {**Falsehood does not approach it (the Qur'an) from before it or from behind.**}[45], and:

{**We have sent down the Reminder and We shall be its protectors.**}[46]

The Integrity of the Qur'an

In our book '*The Ways to the Messages*',[47] we mentioned that the Qur'an, as we can show from evidences and from common sense, has not been subject to any additions or subtractions or any changes or alterations from the way in which the Messenger of Allah (S) organised it during his life even though chronologically some verses were revealed before others. The Qur'an of the time of the Messenger of Allah (S) is exactly the same as that which we have today. The Prophet himself specified the placing of verses and chapters in the way we see now and there are many traditions that testify to this.

It is widely related that the Prophet (S) said: '*Whoever completes a recitation of the Qur'an will receive such and such a reward.*'[48]

Had the Qur'an not been complete then this would not have been possible. The Qur'an was also present at his time in a complete written form in the Prophet's mosque, by the Prophet's pulpit, from which anyone could make a copy.

Also, thousands of Muslims had memorised the entire Qur'an as the chronicles of the time report. In this way the integrity, structure and organisation of the Qur'an remained until this day.

---

[45] *The Qur'an*: Verses Explained (41): 42.
[46] *The Qur'an*: Al-Hijr (15): 9.
[47] *Al-Wasa'il ila al-Rasa'il (The Ways to the Messages)*: vol.2, p.97-100.
[48] *Usul al-Kafi*: vol.2, p.604.

The Qur'an of 'Ali

As for the question of the Qur'an of 'Ali (a) which he presented and was not allowed (by the ruler of the time), what is meant by this are the commentaries and interpretations which he collected and which he himself mentioned in a speech related from him. It is clear that they did not want the commentary or interpretation because it was a special merit of Imam 'Ali's (a).

Also, what is meant by the gathering of the Qur'an by 'Umar or 'Uthman, if this was the case, is that the scattered incomplete documents of the Qur'an written by the companions of the Prophet (S) were brought together so there would not be one complete Qur'an and several incomplete versions. This is a natural thing, for example when the speeches of a lecturer are gathered by his students, some students will be absent for reasons of illness or travel or the like and hence not have the complete versions of the speeches. Those who had a full attendance record however will have the complete version.

'Umar and 'Uthman destroyed the scattered and different documents but not the complete Qur'an from the time of the Prophet (S).

I myself have seen copies of the Qur'an written over one thousand years ago in the cabinet of the Shrine of Imam al-Hussein (a); they were absolutely no different to the Qur'an we have today. There are also a number of copies of the Qur'an written in the hand of the Imams in Iran and 'Iraq and Turkey, all of which are the same as the Qur'an existent today with no changes.

The Different Readings

The 'different readings' are a modern phenomenon that arose from the opinions of a particular group. Muslims at the time of the great reciters and after them did not pay those opinions heed and were not concerned with them so as to change the Qur'an. For this reason, we would consider the prayer of those who practise these 'readings' to be invalid.

The 'Corruption' of the Qur'an in the Traditions

Those traditions that attest to the corruption of the Qur'an which are to be found in the books of the Sunnites and Shi'a alike are spurious and groundless traditions. Upon further examination we found that 90% of these traditions in the books of the Shi'a are related by a man called al-Sayyari who is, by the unanimous opinion of the biographers, a liar, forger of *hadith* and devious. The rest of the traditions have either no valid chain of narration or no proof, as any careful examiner would find out. The Sunnite traditions also show themselves up to be false as is clear to anyone who cares to consult the narrations in the book of al-Bukhari and others.

Part Two

The Qur'an in the Traditions[49]

Learning the Qur'an

The Messenger of Allah (S) said:

> '*There are three groups of people who will not be concerned with the reckoning (on the day of judgement), nor will they fear the shriek (on that day) nor the great consternation: firstly, one who learns the Qur'an and knows it off by heart and acts according to its (teachings) for he will come to Allah as an honoured nobleman, secondly the muethin (he who calls the faithful to prayer) who has practised for seven years and never sought any payment for it, and thirdly the servant who has obeyed Allah and obeyed his master.'* [50]

The Messenger of Allah (S) also said:

> '*Allah rewards the man who kisses his son kindly with a blessing, and he who makes his son happy, Allah makes him happy on the day of resurrection, and he who teaches his son the Qur'an, the parents will be summoned on the day of resurrection and will be clothed in garments whose light illuminates the people of Paradise.'* [51]

---

[49] The traditions on the learning and recitation of the Qur'an is a further evidence that the Holy Qur'an was compiled, and therefore referred to by the Muslims during the lifetime of the Prophet Muhammad, peace be upon him.

[50] *Appendix to The Shi'a Guide to the Shari'a*: vol.4, p.21.

[51] *Seas of Lights*: vol.7, p.304; Al-Kafi: vol.6, p.49.

The Messenger of Allah (S) also said:

> '*This Qur'an is the etiquette of Allah so learn his etiquette as much as you can.*'[52]

He (S) also said:

> '*There is not a single believer, man or woman, freeman or bondman who is exempt from the right that Allah has over him to learn the Qur'an and to study its meanings.* Then he read the following verse: {**Be ye worshippers for you have taught the book . . . }**[53] [54]

He (S) also said:

> '*The best of you is he who learns the Qur'an and teaches it.*'[55]

He (S) also said:

> '*Everything will seek forgiveness for the teacher and the learner of the Qur'an, even the fish in the sea.*'[56]

He (S) also said:

> '*Learn ye the Qur'an, for the similitude of one who carries the Qur'an (in his heart) is he who carries a bag full of musk which when he opens it fills the air with the sent, and if keeps it shut, it keeps the scent of the musk.*[57]

He (S) also said:

> '*One who teaches his child the Qur'an is like one who has made ten thousand Hajj pilgrimages, and ten thousand 'Umrah pilgrimages, and has freed ten thousand slaves of the sons of Ishmael, and fed and clothed ten thousand poor, hungry and unclothed Muslims. For every letter he will receive ten blessings and ten evil deeds of his will be wiped*

---

[52] *Appendix to The Shi'a Guide to the Shari'a*: vol.4, p.232.
[53] *The Qur'an*: The Clan of 'Imran (3): 79.
[54] *Appendix to The Shi'a Guide to the Shari'a*: vol.4, p.232.
[55] *Appendix to The Shi'a Guide to the Shari'a*: vol.4, p.232; Also *The Shi'a Guide to the Shari'a*: vol.4, p.825.
[56] *Appendix to The Shi'a Guide to the Shari'a*: vol.4, p.235.
[57] *Appendix to The Shi'a Guide to the Shari'a*: vol.4, p.246.

> *out, and the Qur'an will be with him in his grave until the day he is resurrected. His balance scales will tip in his favour and he will be taken across the Sirat (the straight path) as quick as lightning and the Qur'an will not leave him until he has reached a station the loftiness of which is more than can be imagined.*[58]

He (S) said also:

> *'Allah will crown the parents of the one who teaches his child the Qur'an with a kingly crown and clothe them in robes the like of which has never been seen before.'*[59]

Related from Amir al-Mu'minin 'Ali Ibn Abu Talib (a) that the Prophet (S) said:

> *'The best of you is the one who learns the Qur'an and teaches it.'*[60]

In one of his speeches contained in the book *Nahj al-Balagha*, Imam 'Ali (a) says:

> *'Learn Ye the Qur'an for it is the best of speech and study it for it is the springtime of the heart. Seek cure by its light for it heals the breast, and make your reading of it beautiful for it is the most beneficial of narratives. The learned man who acts without using his knowledge is as the ignorant, confused man who will never awake from his ignorance, in fact the case against him is greater and loss is more incumbent upon him, and in the sight of Allah he is the most blameworthy.*[61]

Also related from Imam 'Ali (a) is that he said:

> *'If the teacher says to his pupil: Say: 'In the Name of Allah The Beneficent The Merciful.' And the pupil says: 'In The Name of Allah The Beneficent The Merciful.' Then Allah*

---

[58] *Appendix to The Shi'a Guide to the Shari'a*: vol.4, p.247.

[59] *The Shi'a Guide to the Shari'a*: vol.4, p.825.

[60] *Ghawali al-Layali*: vol.1, p.99; Also *Appendix to The Shi'a Guide to the Shari'a*: vol.4, p.235.

[61] *Nahj al-Balagha*: Sermon no.110, paragraph 6; see also *Seas of Lights*: vol.2, p.36.

> *will give absolution to them both and to the pupil's parents.'* [62]

Related from Imam Ja'far al-Saadiq (a) is that he said:

> *'The believer should not die before learning the Qur'an or be in the process of learning it.'* [63]

The Magnificence of the Qur'an

The Messenger of Allah (S) said:

> *'The Qur'an is a guidance from error, an elucidation from blindness, a release from stumbling, a light in the darkness, an illumination from events, a protection from destruction, a guidance against temptations, clarity from trials, and a conveyor from this world unto the next. In it is your complete religion, no-one strays from the Qur'an but into the fire.'* [64]

And he (S) said:

> *'Whoever is given the Qur'an by Allah and thinks that any man has been given anything better than he has been given, then he has diminished a great thing and aggrandised a minor thing.'* [65]

And he (S) said:

> *'The virtue of the Qur'an over the rest of speech is as the virtue of Allah over His creation.'* [66]

And he (S) said:

> *'Allah does not punish the heart which is a vessel for the Qur'an.'* [67]

---

[62] *Jami'a al-Akhbar*: p.42, section 22; and see *Appendix to the Shi'a Guide to the Shari'a*: vol.4, p.387.

[63] 'Iddat al-Da'i: p.287, chapter 6 on the recital of the Qur'an; see also *Usul al-Kafi*: vol.2, p.607.

[64] *Usul al-Kafi*: vol.2, p.600.

[65] *Usul al-Kafi*: vol.2, p.605; *The Shi'a Guide to the Shari'a*: vol.3, p.582.

[66] *Seas of Lights*: vol.89, p.19.

[67] *The Shi'a Guide to the Shari'a*: vol.4, p.825.

And he (S) said:

> *'Whoever makes his speech the Qur'an, and the mosque his house, Allah builds for him a house in paradise.'* [68]

It is related that Abu Dharr came to the Prophet (S) and said:

> *'O Messenger of Allah, I fear lest I should learn the Qur'an and not act according to it.' So the Messenger of Allah (S) said: 'Allah will not punish the heart in which He has made the Qur'an dwell.'* [69]

The Messenger of Allah (S) mentioned commotion one day, so we said: O Messenger of Allah how do we save ourselves from it? He (S) said:

> *'By the book of Allah. In it is news of those who came before you, and news of those to come after you, and a way to judge between yourselves. It is the criterion and it is not in jest. No tyrant will neglect it but his back will be broken by Allah. He who seeks guidance in other than the Qur'an will fall into error. It is the sturdy rope and the wise reminder and the straight path. Tongues cannot obscure it, it does not pall despite much reading, nor do scholars ever tire of it. Its wonders never cease . . .'* [70]

And he (S) said:

> *'The Angel Gabriel descended upon me and said: 'O Muhammad, everything has a master . . ., the master of speech is the Arabic language, and the master of the Arabic language is the Qur'an.'* [71]

Related from Mu'adh b. Jabal who said:

> *'We were travelling with the Messenger of Allah (S) and I said: 'O Messenger of Allah, tell us about what it is that will benefit us.' He (S) said: 'If you desire the life of the felicitous, and the death of the martyrs, and deliverance on the day of the gathering, and the shade on the day of heat,*

---

[68] *Al-Tahdhib*: vol.3, p.255.

[69] *Appendix to The Shi'a Guide to the Shari'a*: vol.4, p.255.

[70] *Appendix to The Shi'a Guide to the Shari'a*: vol.4, p.239.

[71] *Seas of Lights*: vol.61, p.30.

> *and guidance on the day of error, then study the Qur'an for it is the speech of the Most Merciful, and a refuge from Satan, and tips the balance scales in your favour.'* [72]

And he (S) also said:

> *'The Qur'an is better than anything else other than Allah. He who reveres the Qur'an has revered Allah and he who does not revere the Qur'an has made light of the sanctity of Allah. The sanctity of the Qur'an to Allah is as the sanctity of the father to his son.'* [73]

And he (S) said:

> *'It is not proper for one who carries the Qur'an to think that anyone has been given something better than he has been given, for even if he owned the entire world, the Qur'an would be better than what he owned.'* [74]

And he (S) said during the days of his passing from this world, among that which he advised his companions:

> *'The book of Allah and the people of my household. The book of Allah is the Qur'an. In it is the proof, the light and the evidence. It is the speech of Allah, it is live and always valid, and applicable to current issues. Whenever it is read thoughtfully it is always fresh, and it is the witness (upon those concerned). It is a just judge, and it is a reference which can always be referred to. . . . Tomorrow (on the day of judgement) it will confute against groups of people, and their feet would slip off the Sirat (the straight path)* [75].

In a *hadith* from Abu Dharr who said:

> *'I heard the Messenger of Allah (S) saying: 'Looking upon 'Ali b. Abi Talib (a) is an act of worship, as is looking upon one's parents with kindness and mercy. Looking upon a*

---

[72] *Appendix to The Shi'a Guide to the Shari'a*: vol.4, p.232.
[73] *Appendix to The Shi'a Guide to the Shari'a*: vol.4, p.236.
[74] *Appendix to The Shi'a Guide to the Shari'a*: vol.4, p.237.
[75] *Appendix to The Shi'a Guide to the Shari'a*: vol.4, p.237.

> *page from the Qur'an is an act of worship, and looking upon the Ka'bah is an act of worship.'* [76]

Commander of the Faithful, Imam 'Ali (a) says in description of the Qur'an:

> *'. . . Then, Allah sent to him the Book as a light whose flames cannot be extinguished, a lamp whose glow does not die, a sea whose depth cannot be sounded, a way whose direction does not mislead, a ray whose light does not darken, a separator (of good from evil) whose arguments do not weaken, a clarifier whose foundations cannot be dismantled, a cure which leaves no apprehension for disease, an honour whose supporters are not defeated, and a truth whose helpers are not abandoned. Therefore, it is the mine of belief and its centre, the source of knowledge and its oceans, the plantation of justice and its pools, the foundation stone of Islam and its construction, the valleys of truth and its plains. An ocean which those who draw water cannot empty, springs which those who draw water cannot dry up, a watering place which those who come to take water cannot exhaust, a staging place in moving towards which travellers do not get lost, signs which no wayfarer fails to see and a highland which those who approach it cannot surpass it.*
>
> *Allah has made it a quencher of the thirst of the learned, a bloom for the hearts of religious jurists, a highway for the ways of the righteous, a cure after which there is no ailment, an effulgence with which there is no darkness, a rope whose grip is strong, a stronghold whose top is invulnerable, an honour for him who loves it, a peace for him who enters it, a guidance for him who follows it, an excuse for him who adopts it, an argument for him who argues with it, a witness for him who quarrels with it, a success for him who argues with it, a carrier of burden for him who seeks the way, a shield for him who arms himself (against misguidance), a knowledge for him who listens*

---

[76] *Al-Manaqib*: vol.3, p.202; *The Shi'a Guide to the Shari'a*: vol.4, p.854.

> *carefully, a worthy story for him who relates it and a final verdict for him who passes judgements.'* [77]

He (a) also said:

> *'The outer manifestation of the Qur'an is elegant, and the inner meanings of it are deep, its marvels never cease nor do its wonders come to an end, darkness cannot be dispelled except by it.'* [78]

He (a) also said:

> *'Allah has not admonished anyone before with the like of the Qur'an. It is Allah's sturdy rope, and His trustworthy means, in it is the springtime of the hearts, and the founts of knowledge, hearts do not have illumination without it.'* [79]

And he (a) said:

> *'This Qur'an is the counsellor that does not give false counsel, the guide that does not lead astray, and the speaker that does not lie. No-one will sit with this Qur'an but that he stand up from it with an increase and a decrease; an increase in guidance, and a decrease in blindness. Know ye that after knowing the Qur'an, no-one can again experience poverty, neither can anyone before knowing the Qur'an experience riches. Seek ye in it the cure to your ailments, and succour in your hardships. In it is the cure from the greatest of ills, which are unbelief, hypocrisy, blindness, and errancy. Beseech Allah through it, and seek a direction to Him through the love of it, and do not ask of his creation through it. (There is) nothing like it that leads the people to monotheism. Know ye that it is an intercessor whose intercession is accepted, and a speaker which confirms the truth, and that whoever the Qur'an asks intercession for on the day of resurrection will be granted such, and whoever the Qur'an speaks against on the day of resurrection it will speak the truth against him. On the day of resurrection a herald will proclaim: Verily*

---

[77] *Nahj al-Balagha*: Sermon no. 198.
[78] *Seas of Lights*: vol.2, p. 284.
[79] *Seas of Lights*: vol.2, p. 312.

*every ploughman is afflicted in what he sows and the
outcome of his works except in the tilth of the Qur'an. So be
of its tilth and its followers and seek evidence in it about
your Lord, and counsel about yourselves, and question with
it your opinions, and seek to expose with it your vain
desires.'* [80]

From Imam Zayn al-'Abidin (a):

*'The verses of the Qur'an are treasure houses. Therefore
every time you open a treasure house you must look to see
what is in it.'* [81]

And he (a) said:

*'If all the peoples of the east and the west were to die, I
would not feel alone as long as the Qur'an was with me.'* [82]

From Imam al-Baaqir (a) who said:

*'The Commander of the Faithful (a) said: 'Shall I inform
you about the true religious scholar? He is one who does
not invoke in the people a despair of the mercy of Allah,
nor does he invoke in them a sense of security from the
punishment of Allah. He does not give licence to disobeying
Allah and does not neglect the Qur'an seeking other than it.
Indeed there is no good in a knowledge in which there is
not a deep understanding, nor is there any good in a recital
of the Qur'an in which there is no pondering, nor is there
any good in an act of worship in which there is no heartfelt
comprehension.'* [83]

And he (a) said:

*'The Qur'an will arrive on the day of resurrection in the
most beautiful aspect and form. It will pass by the Muslims
and they will say: this man is one of us. Then it will pass
beyond them to the prophets and they will say: he is one of
us. It will then pass beyond them to the Archangels and*

---

[80] *Appendix to The Shi'a Guide to the Shari'a*: vol.4, p.239.
[81] *The Shi'a Guide to the Shari'a*: vol.4, p.849; *Usul al-Kafi*: vol.2, p.609.
[82] *Usul al-Kafi*: vol.2, p.602.
[83] *The Shi'a Guide to the Shari'a*: vol.4, p.829; *Seas of Lights*: vol.2, p.48.

*they will say: he is one of us. Until it ends up before The
Lord of Power, Almighty and Exalted is He, and it will say:
Lord, I made such and such a person thirsty during his
middays, and kept him awake during his nights on Earth.
But I did not make such and such a person thirsty during
his mid-days, and did not keep him awake during his
nights. So Allah Almighty will say: Let them enter the
garden according to their stations. So (the Qur'an) will
arise and they will follow it and it will say to each believer:
Recite and advance. So they recite and advance until each
person has reached his allotted station and has settled
therein.'* *[84]*

Also from Imam al-Baaqir (a) that he said:

*'Learn the Qur'an, for it will come on the day of
resurrection in the most beautiful of forms ever seen by
Allah's creation. There the people will be arrayed in one-
hundred and twenty thousand rows; eighty thousand rows
are the nation of Muhammad (S), and forty thousand rows
for the remainder of the nations. The Qur'an will come to
the ranks of the Muslims in the form of a man. He will greet
them and they will look towards him and say: There is no
god but Allah the Patient the Generous. This man is one of
the Muslims we recognise him by his aspect and character
except that he was of a greater understanding than us in
the Qur'an. Hence he has been given of magnificence,
beauty and light that which we have not been given. Then
he passes on until he comes upon the ranks of the martyrs
who say: There is no god but Allah the Most Merciful Lord.
This man is one of the martyrs, we recognise him by his
features and character except that he is one of the martyrs
of the sea, for it is from there that he has been given of
beauty and virtue that which we have not been given. Then
he passes on until he comes upon the ranks of the martyrs
of the sea in the form of a martyr. The martyrs of the sea
look upon him and their wonderment is great and they say:
This man is of the martyrs of the sea, we recognise him by
his features and character except that the island in which*

---

[84] *Usul al-Kafi*: vol.2, p.601; *The Shi'a Guide to the Shari'a*: vol.4, p.824.

he met his end was more fearful than the island in which we met our ends. Hence he has been given of magnificence, beauty and light that which we have not been given. Then he passes on until he comes upon the ranks of the prophets and messengers in the form of a prophet and messenger. The prophets and messengers look upon him and great is their wonderment of him and they say: There is no god but Allah the Magnificent the Esteemed. This is a prophet and messenger, we recognise him by his character and features except that he has been given a great bounty. They then gather together and approach the Messenger of Allah (S) and ask him: O Muhammad! Who is this man? He says: Do you not recognise him? They say: We do not recognise him, he is one that has not the wrath of Allah upon him. The Messenger of Allah (S) says: This is the proof of Allah upon his creation. So he gives a greeting of peace, and passes on until he reaches the ranks of the Angels in the form of an Archangel. The Angels look upon him and great becomes their wonderment until it becomes too much for them for what they see of his virtue. They say: Exalted is our Lord and Most Holy, this servant is one of the Angels, we recognise him by his features and character except that he is the most near of the Angels in station to Allah The Most Powerful and Majestic. Hence he has been attired in light and beauty.' [85]

Imam al-Saadiq (a) said:

'Among that which the Commander of the Faithful (a) enjoined upon his companions was that he said: 'Know Ye that the Qur'an is the guidance during the night and the day, and the light during the dark night over exertion and poverty.' [86]

And he (a) said:

'In this Qur'an there is the beacon of guidance and the lanterns of darkness . . . Therefore he who wants to polish

---

[85] *Seas of Lights*: vol.7, p.319; *Usul al-Kafi*: vol.2, p.596.
[86] *Seas of Lights*: vol.65, p.212; *Usul al-Kafi*: vol.2, p.216.

> *his eyes (to see the truth) he should open his sight to the light (of the Qur'an) . . . since reflecting and thinking is the life of the heart of the wise, just as the one with a torch of light who walks in darkness.*[87]

A man questioned Imam al-Saadiq (a) and said:

> *'What is it with the Qur'an that despite the propagation and studying of it, it only increases in freshness? So he said (a): 'It is that Allah, Blessed and Exalted is He, has not made the Qur'an for one specific era rather than another, or for one group of people rather than another. Therefore, in every time it is new and amongst every people is fresh until the day of resurrection.'*[88]

He (a) also said:

> *'That Allah Blessed and Exalted is He, revealed in the Qur'an an exposition of every thing, so that He has not neglected anything needed by his servants, and so that no servant is able to say: if only such and such a subject was in the Qur'an, but that Allah has sent down revelation about that subject in it.*[89]

He (a) said:

> *'Then the Qur'an ends up standing to the right of the throne and The Omnipotent will say: By My Greatness and My Majesty, and the Exaltedness of My Station, I will indeed honour today those who have honoured you and I will humiliate those who have belittled you.'*[90]

He (a) said:

> *'The Qur'an is a prohibitor and an orderer; it orders to paradise and prohibits from the fire.'*[91]

He (a) said:

---

[87] *Usul al-Kafi*: vol.2, p.200; *The Shi'a Guide to the Shari'a*: vol.4, p.828.

[88] *Seas of Lights*: vol.2, p.280.

[89] *Usul al-Kafi*: vol.1, p.59.

[90] *Usul al-Kafi*: vol.2, p.602; *The Shi'a Guide to the Shari'a*: vol.4, p.827.

[91] *Usul al-Kafi*: vol.2, p.601.

> *'The Qur'an is riches, there are no riches without knowledge of it and no poverty after knowledge of it.'* [92]

From Imam al-Saadiq (a) from his forefathers (a):

> *'The Messenger of Allah (S) said: 'When trials and temptations descend upon you like the darkness of the night, then look to the Qur'an for it is an intercessor whose intercession will be accepted, and a schemer who confirms the truth. He who keeps it in front of him will be lead by it into paradise, he who puts it behind him will be driven into the fire. It is the guide to the best path, and a book in which is explanation, exposition, and learning. It is decisive and not in jest. It has an outside and an inside, its exterior is judgement, and its interior is knowledge, its outer manifestation is elegant and its inner meanings are deep. (when it is studied) Truth and wisdom stems from it. And every truth leads to even more wisdom. Its marvels are without number, and its wonders never cease. The lanterns of guidance, and the lighthouse of wisdom, and the guide to knowledge. Therefore he who wants to polish his eyes (to see the truth), and attain serenity in his vision, and he who wants to release himself from impaired vision and entanglement of the mind, let him use the Qur'an. For thought and reflection gives life to the heart of the wise, just as the one who walks in darkness with a torch. Therefore it is upon you to make sure to rescue yourselves in the best possible way and in the shortest possible time.* [93]

And from Imam al-Saadiq (a) from his father who said:

> *'Indeed it is a source of wonderment to me that there is in a house a copy of the Qur'an with which Allah Almighty is He expels the Satans.'* [94]

From Imam al-Ridha (a) that he mentioned the Qur'an and said:

> *'It is the sturdy rope of Allah and His firm grip, and His perfect road that leads to paradise, and delivers from the*

---

[92] *Jami' al-Akhbar*: p.40; *Tafsir Majma' al-Bayan*: vol.1, p.15.

[93] *The Shi'a Guide to the Shari'a*: vol.4, p.828.

[94] *Thawab al-A'mal*: p.103; *The Shi'a Guide to the Shari'a*: vol.4, p.855.

fire. It does not pall despite the passing of aeons, and does not dissipate despite being oft repeated, because it was not created for one time rather than another but as the argument and proof for all humanity. Falsehood does not approach it from before it or behind it, a revelation from The All Wise, The All Praised.' [95]

The Bearers of the Qur'an

The Messenger of Allah (S) said:

> *'The people of the Qur'an are the people of Allah and His elect.'* [96]

He (S) also said:

> *'The nobles of my nation are those who bear the Qur'an (in their hearts), and the people of the night (who worship Allah during the hours of darkness).* [97]

He (S) also said:

> *'The people of the Qur'an have reached the highest degree of all the children of Adam, apart from the prophets and messengers. Therefore do not deny them their rights for they have from Allah The Almighty a lofty station.'* [98]

He (S) also said:

> *'The person with the most right to humility both secret and public is the bearer of the Qur'an, as is he the person with the most right to prayer and fasting both secret and public.' Then he called at the top of his voice: 'O bearer of the Qur'an, practise humility, with the Qur'an Allah raises you up, and do not make it a source of pride so that Allah humiliates you. O bearer of the Qur'an, beautify yourselves with it for Allah, He will beautify you, but do not beautify yourselves with it for the people that Allah may disgrace*

---

[95] *Seas of Lights*: vol.17, p.210.

[96] *Ghurar al-Hikam wa Durar al-Kilam*: p.111; *Tafsir Majma' al-Bayan*: vol.1, p.15.

[97] *Al-Amali of al-Sheikh al-Suduq*: p.234; *He who is not in the presence of a Jurist*: vol.4, p.499.

[98] *Usul al-Kafi*: vol.2, p.603.

you with it. The person who completes a reading of the Qur'an is as one who has reached the station of prophethood except that he will not receive revelation, and he who upholds the Qur'an, and encourages others to do so, he would not respond in the same way when he is insulted, angered, or wrathed, but he would forgive, pardon and forbear (the offending person) in line with the teaching and the honour of the Qur'an. He who is given the Qur'an and thinks that anyone else has been given something better than he has been given has aggrandised that which Allah has belittled and belittled that which Allah has aggrandised.' [99]

He (S) also said:

'The most honourable of servants in the sight of Allah after the prophets are the scholars, then the bearers of the Qur'an, they will exit from this world as the prophets exit and will be gathered from their tombs with the prophets, and pass over the path along with the prophets and will receive the reward of the prophets. So act kindly with students and bearers of the Qur'an because of the honour and nobility they enjoy in the sight of Allah.' [100]

He (S) also said:

'The bearers of the Qur'an are favoured with the mercy of Allah, they are clothed in the light of Allah, taught the speech of Allah, and drawn near to Allah.' [101]

He (S) also said:

'The bearers of the Qur'an are surrounded by the mercy of Allah, clothed in the light of Allah, taught the speech of Allah. Whoever takes them as an enemy has taken Allah as an enemy, and whoever takes them as a friend has taken Allah as a friend.' [102]

---

[99] *Usul al-Kafi*: vol.2, p.604.

[100] *Appendix to The Shi'a Guide to the Shari'a*: vol.4, p.244.

[101] *Seas of Lights*: vol.89, p.182.

[102] *Appendix to The Shi'a Guide to the Shari'a*: vol.4, p.244.

From the Commander of the Faithful (a) in a noble hadith in description of his followers:

> '. . . During the night they are busy performing the prayers, reading the Qur'an and reciting it, admonishing themselves with its parables, and seeking a cure for their ills with its remedy.' [103]

Also from him (a) that he said:

> 'The bearers of the Qur'an in this world are the wise men of the people of paradise on the day of resurrection.' [104]

The Recitation of the Qur'an

The Messenger of Allah (S) said:

> 'Illuminate your houses with the recitation of the Qur'an.' [105]

He (S) also said:

> 'There are three kinds of people who will be on a dune of musk who will not be saddened by the great terror nor distressed by the reckoning: A man who reads the Qur'an seeking a reward in the hereafter, then leads a people seeking the reward of the hereafter . . .' [106]

He (S) also said:

> 'This Qur'an is the rope of Allah and is the elucidating light, and the beneficial cure . . . So recite it and Allah will reward you for every letter you recite with ten blessings,

---

[103] *Appendix to The Shi'a Guide to the Shari'a*: vol.4, p.240.

[104] *Jami' al-Akhbar*: p.48; See also *Appendix to The Shi'a Guide to the Shari'a*: vol.11, p.7: In which is found: '*The Messenger of Allah (S) said: 'The bearers of the Qur'an are the wise men of the people of Paradise, and those who strive in the way of Allah are their leaders, and the messengers are the masters of the people of Paradise.*'

[105] *Usul al-Kafi*: vol.2, p.610.

[106] *Seas of Lights*: vol.7, p.149.

and I do not say that reciting 'A.L.M' is ten but for 'A' ten, for 'L' ten, and for 'M' ten.' [107]

He said (S):

'O Salman, you must recite the Qur'an, for the recitation of it is an effacement of sins, and a shield from the fire, and a sanctuary from the torment. For every verse one recites, the reward of that of one-hundred martyrs is written for him, and for every chapter he is given the reward of that of a prophet, and the mercy of Allah will descend upon him.' [108]

He (S) also said:

'You must recite the Qur'an, and remember Allah frequently, for it is a remembrance for you in the sky and a light for you on the Earth'. [109]

He (S) said:

'The parents of the reciter of the Qur'an will be crowned with the crown of nobility whose light illuminates for ten thousand years (of walking) distance, and will be clothed in a garment the smallest thread of which will be worth more than one-hundred thousand times those of the earthly world and whatever riches and opulence in it. Then the reciter will be given dominion in his right hand and everlasting life in his left hand in a book which he will read from his right hand: You have been made one of the most esteemed kings of the gardens of heaven and one of the companions of Muhammad (S) Master of the prophets, and 'Ali (a) the best of vice-regents and after them the Imams (a), the pinnacles of piety. He will then read from the book in his left hand: You are safe from separation from this dominion and you have been rescued from death and sickness. You

---

[107] *Jami' al-Akhbar*: p.40; See also *Appendix to The Shi'a Guide to the Shari'a*: vol.24, p.258: In which is found: *'This Qur'an is the rope of Allah and the elucidating light and the beneficial cure so recite it for Allah Exalted is He will reward you for every letter recited with ten blessings. I do not say that A.L.M is all one letter but A and L and M counts as thirty blessings.'*

[108] *Appendix to The Shi'a Guide to the Shari'a*: vol.4, p.257.

[109] *Seas of Lights*: vol.74, p.74.

> *are spared from disease and illness and have avoided the envy of the envious and the schemes of the schemers. Then it will be said to him: Recite and rise to your allotted station at the last verse of the Qur'an you are able to recite. When his parents see their garments and their crowns they will say: Lord, how is it that we have this honour when our acts did not deserve it. They will be told: Almighty Allah has bestowed this upon you for teaching your son the Qur'an.'* [110]

He said (S):

> *'The hearts of men can become rusty just as iron rusts. He was asked: O Messenger of Allah what is their polish? He (S) said: The recitation of the Qur'an and remembrance of death.'* [111]

And he said (S):

> *'Whoever reads the Qur'an seeking Allah and a knowledge of the religion will have a reward the same as will be given to the Angels and the Prophets and Messengers.'* [112]

Amir al-Mu'minin 'Ali ibn Abi Talib (a) said in his will to his son Muhammad ibn al-Hanafiyya:

> *'Know that for the Muslim there are two magnanimities. The one while at home and the ideal during travel. The ideal when at home is the recitation of the Qur'an . . .'* [113]

Imam Hassan (a) said:

> *'He who recites the Qur'an will have his wish granted sooner or later.'* [114]

Imam Zayn al-'Abidin (a) said:

> *'You must heed the Qur'an, for Allah has created the garden of Paradise out of bricks of gold and silver held together with a plaster of musk, where the earth is of*

---

[110] *Seas of Lights*: vol.7, p.208.

[111] *Appendix to The Shi'a Guide to the Shari'a*: vol.2, p.104.

[112] *Seas of Lights*: vol.76, p.372.

[113] *Seas of Lights*: vol.1, p.200.

[114] *Appendix to The Shi'a Guide to the Shari'a*: vol.4, p.260.

> *saffron and the pebbles are of pearl. The stations of the garden are equal to the number of verses of the Qur'an and whoever recites the Qur'an will be told 'Recite and ascend.' Of whoever enters Paradise no-one shall be in a higher station than the reciter of the Qur'an except the Prophets and the Righteous.* [115]

Related from Imam Baaqir (a) who said:

> *'Everything has a springtime, and the springtime of the Qur'an is the holy month of Ramadan.'* [116]

Related from Imam al-Saadiq (a) who said:

> *'If one reads the Qur'an in his youth as a true believer, the Qur'an mingles with and becomes a part of his flesh and blood, and Allah places him alongside the pious and noble scribes, and on the day of resurrection the Qur'an will be a witness in his favour saying: 'O Lord, every doer of deeds has received the reward for his deeds except for him whose work was with me, so let him have the noblest of your gifts. Then Allah Almighty will clothe him in two of the robes of Paradise and the crown of honour will be placed upon his head. Then the Qur'an will be asked: 'Is this to your satisfaction?' And the Qur'an will answer: 'O Lord I desire for him something better than this.' So he will be given sanctity in his right hand and everlasting life in his left then he will be ushered into Paradise and will be told: 'Recite a verse and for every verse ascend a station.' Then the Qur'an will be asked: 'Have We treated him to your satisfaction?' The Qur'an will answer 'Yes.' (The narrator said):'Whoever recites a great amount of the Qur'an and underwent hardship due to the difficulty of memorisation will be given by Allah this twice over.'* [117]

Also related from Imam al-Saadiq (a):

> *'The best worship is the recitation of the Qur'an.'* [118]

---

[115] *Seas of Lights*: vol.8, p.133.

[116] *The Shi'a Guide to the Shari'a*: vol.4, p.853.

[117] *Thawab al-A'mal*: p.100; and see *Seas of Lights*: vol.7, p.305.

[118] *The Shi'a Guide to the Shari'a*: vol.4, p.825; *Tafsir Majma' al-Bayan*: vol.1, p.15.

And:

> 'Whoever reads the Qur'an in order to learn it by heart, Allah will allow him to enter the garden and his intercession will be accepted for ten of his family who had deserved the fire.' [119]

Also from Imam al-Saadiq (a):

> 'Whoever recites the Qur'an to extract money from the people will arrive on the day of resurrection and his face will be a skull with no flesh on it.' [120]

Related from Imam al-Saadiq (a) from the will of the Prophet (S) to Imam 'Ali (a):

> 'You must recite the Qur'an in all circumstances.' [121]

Also related from him (a):

> 'The house in which there is a Muslim who reads the Qur'an will glitter for the people of the heavens as the star glitters for the people of the earth.' [122]

He said (a):

> 'Amir al-Mu'minin (a) said: 'The house in which the Qur'an is recited and the name of Allah is oft remembered will receive great blessings and will be visited by the Angels and avoided by the demons. It will illuminate for the people of the heavens as the evening star does for the people of the earth. But the house in which the Qur'an is not read nor the name of Allah mentioned will receive few blessings and the Angels will flee from it and the demons will visit it.' [123]

He said (a):

---

[119] *The Shi'a Guide to the Shari'a*: vol.4, p.826; *Tafsir Majma' al-Bayan*: vol.1, p.16.
[120] *Thawab al-A'mal*: p.279.
[121] *The Shi'a Guide to the Shari'a*: vol.4, p.839; *Seas of Lights*: vol.74, p.70.
[122] *'Iddat al-Da'i*: p.287; and see *Usul al-Kafi*: vol.2, p.610.
[123] *'Iddat al-Da'i*: p.247; and see *Usul al-Kafi*: vol.2, p.498.

> *'Whoever reads the Qur'an from the Holy text will find gratification for the eye, and the torment will be lessened for his parents even if they were disbelievers.'* [124]

He (a) said:

> *'One who reads the Qur'an has riches beyond which there is no poverty and if he does not read then there is no way to riches.'* [125]

And related from him (a):

> *'The houses in which prayer is held at night with the recitation of the Qur'an will illuminate for the people of the heavens as the stars illuminate for the people of the earth.'* [126]

He (a) said:

> *'The reciter of the Qur'an who does not subjugate to Allah and whose heart does not soften and who does not cover himself with sadness and dread in secret has belittled the greatness of Allah Almighty is He and is in manifest loss. The reciter of the Qur'an requires three things: A fearful heart, (being) away from any distraction and a place free of others.'* [127]

He (a) said:

> *'By Allah, there is not a single of our followers who recite the Qur'an in their prayers standing but that they will be given for every letter one-hundred blessings, or in their prayers sitting but that they will be given for every letter fifty blessings, and at times other than in prayer but that they will be given for every letter ten blessings.'* [128]

He (a) said:

---

[124] *The Shi'a Guide to the Shari'a*: vol.4, p.853; *Usul al-Kafi*: vol.2, p.613; and *Thawab al-A'mal*: p.102.

[125] *Usul al-Kafi*: vol.2, p.605.

[126] *He who is not in the presence of a Jurist*: vol.1, p.473.

[127] *Appendix to The Shi'a Guide to the Shari'a*: vol.4, p.240.

[128] *Seas of Lights*: vol.65, p.81.

> *'There are three types of Qur'anic reciters. There is the reciter who seeks to impress patrons and attain power over the people and he is destined for the fire. Then there is the reciter who reads the Qur'an and memorises its letters but neglects to act within its laws and he is destined for the fire. Then there is the reciter who reads and hides himself with the Qur'an under his cloak and he acts according to the clear verses and has faith in the ambiguous verses, he establishes its injunctions, makes lawful what it makes lawful and prohibits what it makes unlawful. This is one whom Allah has rescued from the trials which lead astray and he is of the people of Paradise and his intercession will be accepted for whomsoever he wishes.'* [129]

He (a) said:

> *'What is there to prevent the traders amongst you when you come back home from work to read a chapter of the Qur'an before sleep? For each verse you read you will be accredited with ten good deeds and ten foul deeds will be erased.'* [130]

He (a) said:

> *'The faithful son of Adam (a) will be summoned for the reckoning and the Qur'an will go before him in the most beautiful of aspects and say: 'O Lord, I am the Qur'an and this is your faithful servant who used to tire himself by reciting me and to spend long nights reading me and his eyes would stream when he spent the nights in prayer, so please him as he has pleased me.' Allah Almighty will say: 'Open your right hand, then he will fill it with the pleasure of Allah Almighty and he will fill his left hand with the mercy of Allah then he will be told: 'This garden of Paradise is open to you so recite and ascend. For every verse he recites he will ascend a station.'* [131]

He (a) said:

---

[129] *Seas of Lights*: vol.89, p.179.
[130] *Seas of Lights*: vol.89, p.202.
[131] *Seas of Lights*: vol.7, p.267.

'The Qur'an is the covenant of Allah to his creation therefore it is imperative that the Muslim should look into this covenant and read from it each day fifty verses.' [132]

In the book 'The Reliance of the Summoner to Faith', Imam Ali al-Ridha (a) quotes the Prophet (S) who said:

'Give your houses some benefit from the Qur'an, for the house in which the Qur'an is recited brings ease, and plenty for those who dwell in it and if the Qur'an is not recited in it then it will become difficult for the household and they will be in need.' [133]

He (a) said:

'It is incumbent for the man when he awakes in the morning after his prayer to read fifty verses of the Qur'an.' [134]

Related from al-Hassan al-Askari (a) who said:

'The opening surah of the book is the most noble of the jewels of the exalted throne of Allah . . . and whoever reads it while offering allegiance to Muhammad and his family, Allah will give him for every letter a reward each one of which is better than all the wealth of the world and its fineries. The same will be given to the one who listens to the recitation. So make sure you do this often.' [135]

The Reciters of the Qur'an

Related from Imam Baaqir (a) who said:

'Reciters of the Qur'an are of three types: A man who recites the Qur'an and takes it as if a thing for sale and seeks to impress patrons and gain power over the people. Then there is the man who recites the Qur'an and learns its words by heart but forgets to act within the bounds of its

---

[132] *Usul al-Kafi*: vol.2, p.609.

[133] *'Iddat al-Da'i*: p.278; and see *The Shi'a Guide to the Shari'a*: vol.4, p.850.

[134] *Al-Tahdhib*: vol.2, p.138; and see *The Shi'a Guide to the Shari'a*: vol.4, p.849.

[135] *'Uyun Akhbar al-Rida*: vol.1, p.302; and *Tafsir al-Imam Hasan al-'Askari(a)*: p.29.

laws . . . and may Allah not make these types of bearers of the Qur'an proliferate. Then there is the man who recites the Qur'an and cures his ailing heart with the Qur'an's antidote. He remains awake at night with it and goes thirsty during his days to be with it and stands up with it in his place of prayer and leaves his bed to be with it. It is because of them that Almighty Allah will restrain the calamity and grant victory over the enemy, and grant blessed rain from the heavens. I swear by Allah that these among the reciters of the Qur'an are rarer than red sulphur.' [136]

Related from al-Saadiq (a) from his forefathers who said:

'The Messenger of Allah (S) said: 'There are two sections of the Islamic Ummah who if they are righteous then the Ummah will be righteous and if corrupt then the Ummah will be corrupt – the commanders and the Qur'anic reciters.' [137]

How to Read the Qur'an

The Messenger of Allah (S) said:

'The beautiful voice is the adornment of the Qur'an.' [138]

He (S) said:

'The Archangel Gabriel ordered me to read the Qur'an while standing.' [139]

He (S) said:

'The Qur'an descended with sadness. Therefore, if you read it then weep and if you cannot weep then feign weeping. [140]

---

[136] *Usul al-Kafi*: vol.2, p.627; *Al-Khisal*: p.42; and *Seas of Lights*: vol.89, p.178.

[137] *Al-Amali of al-Sheikh al-Suduq*: p.366; *Appendix to The Shi'a Guide to the Shari'a*: vol.4, p.253.

[138] *Appendix to The Shi'a Guide to the Shari'a*: vol.4, p.273.

[139] *Appendix to The Shi'a Guide to the Shari'a*: vol.4, p.427.

[140] *Appendix to The Shi'a Guide to the Shari'a*: vol.4, p.270.

And he (S) said:

> '*Beautify the Qur'an with your voices for the beautiful voice increases the beauty of the Qur'an.*' [141]

In al-Khisal with a chain of transmitters from 'Ali (a) who said:

> '*The servant of Allah should not recite the Qur'an if he is not in a state of ritual purity until he purifies himself.*' [142]

Related from Imam al-Saadiq (a) who said:

> '*The Qur'an descended with sadness so recite it with sadness.*' [143]

And related from Imam al-Saadiq (a) who said:

> '*The Messenger of Allah (S) said: 'Recite ye the Qur'an with the voice and tone of the Arabs and avoid the tone of those who practise foul deeds and great sins. There will come a people after me who will sing the Qur'an in the style of popular song or the style of the monks or as a lamentation . . .their hearts will be tried as will those who are enamoured by what they do.*' [144]

He (a) said:

> '*The Prophet (S) said: 'Everything has an adornment and the adornment of the Qur'an is the beautiful voice.*' [145]

Also related from him (a):

> '*Learn ye the Arabic language for it is the speech of Allah with which he addressed his creation and spoke with it to the ancients.*' [146]

It is related that Imam al-Kaadhem (a) had a beautiful voice and that he excelled in the recital of the Qur'an. It is related that Imam Zayn

---

[141] *Appendix to The Shi'a Guide to the Shari'a*: vol.4, p.273.
[142] *Al-Khisal*: p.627; and see *The Shi'a Guide to the Shari'a*: vol.4, p.847.
[143] *The Shi'a Guide to the Shari'a*: vol.4, p.857; and see *Usul al-Kafi*: vol.2, p.614.
[144] *The Shi'a Guide to the Shari'a*: vol.4, p.857; and see *Usul al-Kafi*: vol.2, p.614.
[145] *The Shi'a Guide to the Shari'a*: vol.4, p.859; and see *Usul al-Kafi*: vol.2, p.615.
[146] *The Shi'a Guide to the Shari'a*: vol.3, p.398; and see *Seas of Lights*: vol.73, p.127.

el-Abidin (a) was reading the Qur'an and if a passer by heard him he would be astounded at the beauty of his voice.' [147]

Related from Imam al-Ridha (a) who said:

> 'The Messenger of Allah said: 'Beautify the Qur'an with your voices for the beautiful voice can only enhance the beauty of the Qur'an.' [148]

The Memorisation of the Qur'an

The Messenger of Allah (S) said:

> 'The number of stations in the garden of Paradise corresponds to the number of verses of the Qur'an. When someone who knows the Qur'an enters the garden he will be told: 'Recite and for every verse ascend a station.' There will be no station higher than he who has memorised the entire Qur'an.' [149]

Related from Imam al-Saadiq (a) who said:

> 'The person who has memorised the Qur'an and acts in accordance with it will be counted among the noble and pious.' [150]

He (a) also said:

> 'How important is the Qur'an! Each verse and each chapter of the Qur'an will arrive on the day of resurrection and will rise one thousand stations illuminating the garden and will say: If only you had memorised me I would have brought you here. [151]

Also related from Imam al-Saadiq (a):

---

[147] *Appendix to The Shi'a Guide to the Shari'a*: vol.4, p.274.
[148] *'Uyun Akhbar al-Rida*: vol.2, p.322; *The Shi'a Guide to the Shari'a*: vol.4, p.859.
[149] *Appendix to The Shi'a Guide to the Shari'a*: vol.4, p.231.
[150] *Thawab al-A'mal*: p.101; *Seas of Lights*: vol.56, p.171; *Seas of Lights*: vol.89, p.177.
[151] *Usul al-Kafi*: vol.2, p.608.

43

> '*The person who takes pains to memorise the Qur'an through his own labours although his memory be weak will gain twice the reward.*' [152]

He (a) said:

> '*Whoever forgets a chapter of the Qur'an will see that chapter in the most beautiful of aspects and the most lofty of stations in the garden. When he sees it he will say: What are you? How beautiful you are. I wish you were for me. The chapter will say: Do you not recognise me? I am such and such a chapter of the Qur'an. If you had not forgotten me I would have raised you to this station.*' [153]

Related from Imam Kaadhem (a):

> '*The stations of the garden of Paradise are the same number as the verses of the Qur'an and it will be said: Recite and ascend. So he will read and ascend.*' [154]

Listening to the Qur'an

The Messenger of Allah (S) said:

> '*The evils of this world will be repelled from one who listens to the Qur'an and the calamity of the next world will be repelled from the reciter of the Qur'an. Listening to a single verse of the book of Allah is better than a great amount of gold, and reciting a verse from the book of Allah is better than what is below the heavenly throne to the nether regions of the Earth.*' [155]

He (S) also said:

---

[152] *Seas of Lights*: vol.89, p.202.

[153] *Thawab al-A'mal*: p.238; and see *Al-Mahasin*: p.96.

[154] *The Shi'a Guide to the Shari'a*: vol.4, p.840; see also *Thawab al-A'mal*: p.129 in which is found: '*The degrees of Paradise are equal to the number of Qur'anic verses. The reciter of the Qur'an will be told 'recite and ascend!'*'

[155] *Appendix to The Shi'a Guide to the Shari'a*: vol.4, p.261.

> *'The reciter of the Qur'an and the one who listens are equal in their reward.'* [156]

Related from Imam Zayn al-'Abidin (a) who said:

> *'Whoever listens to a letter from the book of Allah without reading it will revive the reward of a good deed and an evil deed of his will be erased and he will rise a degree in station. Whoever reads the book of Allah while looking at it in other than during the ritual prayers, Allah will write for him for every letter a good deed and erase an evil deed, and raise him a degree in station. Whoever learns a letter from the book of Allah, Allah will write in his record ten good deeds, and erase ten evil deeds and raise him ten degrees. I do not say: For every verse but for every letter. Whoever reads a letter while sitting in prayer, Allah will write in his record fifty good deeds and erase fifty evil deeds and will raise him fifty degrees. Whoever reads a letter while standing in prayer, Allah will write in his record one-hundred good deeds and erase one-hundred of his evil deeds and raise him one-hundred degrees in station. Whoever completes a recitation of the book of Allah his wish will be granted sooner or later.'* [157]

Imam Saadiq (a) was asked:

> *'Is it incumbent upon one who hears someone reciting the Qur'an to listen and pay heed to him?'* He said: *'Yes, If the Qur'an is recited near you, you should listen to it.'* [158]

Abandoning the Qur'an

The Messenger of Allah (S) said:

> *'There will come a time for my nation when nothing will remain of the Qur'an but its script.'* [159]

---

[156] *Appendix to The Shi'a Guide to the Shari'a*: vol.4, p.261.
[157] See *'Iddat al-Da'i*: p.285-288.
[158] *The Shi'a Guide to the Shari'a*: vol.4, p.861; and see *Appendix to the Shi'a Guide to the Shari'a*: vol.4, p.275. (with a slight difference in wording).
[159] *Seas of Lights*: vol.2, p.109.

He (S) said in his will:

> 'O 'Ali, In Hell there is a millstone of iron with which the heads of the criminal reciters and scholars will be pulverised.' [160]

He (S) said:

> 'Many a reciter of the Qur'an and the Qur'an will curse him.' [161]

He (S) said:

> 'Whoever learns the Qur'an then forgets it on purpose will meet Allah Almighty on the day of resurrection in chains and for every (forgotten) verse there will be a serpent assigned to oversee him. Whoever learns the Qur'an and does not act accordingly preferring to it the love of this world and its vain ornament will deserve the contempt of Allah and will be in the lowest level (of hell) .....'

He (S) said:

> 'Whoever reads the Qur'an desiring reputation and showing off for the people will meet Allah on the day of resurrection with his face in darkness with no flesh on his face. Whoever reads the Qur'an and does not act accordingly will be brought before Allah on the day of resurrection blind. He will say: 'O Lord, why have I been brought before you blind when I used to see?' He will be told: 'This is the way you approached our verses so that you forgot them, so likewise you are today forgotten.' Then he will be ordered into the fire. Whoever reads the Qur'an desiring reputation, or as a way to argue with the foolish people or to impress the scholars, or seeking through it the things of this world will have his bones scattered by the Almighty on the day of resurrection and no-one in the fire shall have a worse punishment than him and he will be

---

[160] *Appendix to the Shi'a Guide to the Shari'a:* vol.4, p.249.
[161] *Appendix to the Shi'a Guide to the Shari'a:* vol.4, p.249.

> *spared from no kind of torment because of the intensity of the anger and contempt that Allah has for him.* ' [162]

And he (S) said:

> *'The marks of a tyrant are four in number: Disobedience of the Most Merciful, causing hurt to neighbours, hatred of the Qur'an, and nearness to wrongdoing.* ' [163]

Related from Imam Saadiq (a) who said:

> *'There are three things which complain to Allah the Almighty: A dilapidated mosque which is not prayed in by its people, a learned person in the midst of the ignorant, and a copy of the Qur'an left unread on a shelf gathering dust.* ' [164]

The Qur'an and the People of the Prophet's Household

The Most noble Prophet, Muhammad (S) said:

> *'Who loveth Allah then let him love me, and who loveth me let him love my family. I leave behind with you the two momentous things; the book of Allah and my family and who loveth my family then let him love the Qur'an.* ' [165]

He (S) also said:

> *' . . .they (the people of the prophet's household) are with the Qur'an and the Qur'an is with them. They will not deviate from it until they reach me at the sacred well (in Paradise).* ' [166]

He (S) said:

---

[162] *Seas of Lights*: vol.7, p.215.

[163] *Seas of Lights*: vol.1, p.122.

[164] *The Shi'a Guide to the Shari'a*: vol.4, p.855; and see *Usul al-Kafi*: vol.2, p.613.

[165] *Appendix to the Shi'a Guide to the Shari'a*: vol.3, p.355.

[166] *Seas of Lights*: vol.22, p.150.

> '*Ali is with the Qur'an and the Qur'an is with him. They will never diverge until they reach me at the sacred well (of Kawthar in Paradise).*' [167]

He (S) said:

> '*Allah Almighty has favoured the Qur'an and the knowledge of its interpretation and His mercy and divine favour for the allies of Muhammad and his pure family and those who oppose their enemies.*' [168]

Related from Umm Salmah who said:

> '*I heard the Messenger of Allah (S) saying, during the illness which ended in his death and when the room was full of his companions: 'O people, shortly I will die and I will be taken away and I have discharged my duty that I leave with you the two momentous things: the book of my Lord and my family my household. Then he took the hand of 'Ali (a) and said: ' 'Ali is with the Qur'an and the Qur'an is with 'Ali − two successors of insight they will never depart from one another until they reach me at the sacred well*' [169]

Imam 'Ali (a) said:

> '*Allah Almighty purified us and restrained us from sin and made us witnesses over his creation and his proof on the earth. He made us be with the Qur'an and the Qur'an with us. We will never depart from it and it will never depart from us.*' [170]

He (a) said:

> '*We the people of the household cannot be compared to anyone. The Qur'an was revealed amongst us and the mine of the prophetic mission is amongst us.*' [171]

Imam Zayn al-'Abidin (a) said:

---

[167] *Seas of Lights*: vol.38, p.38.

[168] *Seas of Lights*: vol.1, p.217.

[169] *Seas of Lights*: vol.89, p.80.

[170] *Usul al-Kafi*: vol.1, p.191.

[171] *Seas of Lights*: vol.26, p.269.

'Our similitude in the book of Allah is as a niche in which there is a lamp. In the lamp there is a glass and the glass is Muhammad (S) as if he was a pearly star lit from a blessed tree. He said: 'Ali is its oil neither of the East nor of the West. Its oil almost illuminates although no flame has touched it. The Qur'an is light upon light. Allah guides to His light who He wishes, He guides to our allegiance whoever He loves.' [172]

Related from Imam Baaqir (a) regarding Allah's words:

{ then ask the people of al-Dhikr if you do not know.} [173]
He said: *'al-Dhikr is the Qur'an and we are its people.'* [174]

Also related from Imam Baaqir (a):

'The Qur'an was sent down in four quarters; a quarter about us, a quarter about our enemies, a quarter about injunctions and laws, and a quarter traditions and parables. We have the noble parts of the Qur'an.' [175]

He (a) said:

'The Messenger of Allah (S) said: 'I am the first to go before The Almighty on the day of resurrection along with His book and the people of my household. Then will come my nation, then I will ask them what they did with the book of Allah and the people of my household.' [176]

He (a) said regarding the words of Allah:

{We will settle your affairs O ye two momentous things.} [177] *'The two momentous things are the Qur'an and Us.'* [178]

He (a) said:

'Allah has made our regency the axis of the Qur'an.' [179]

---

[172] *Seas of Lights*: vol.23, p.311.
[173] *The Qur'an*: The Bee (16):43.
[174] *Seas of Lights*: vol.23, p.181.
[175] *Seas of Lights*: vol.89, p.114.
[176] *The Shi'a Guide to the Shari'a*: vol.4, p.828.
[177] *The Qur'an*: The Beneficent One (55):31.
[178] *Seas of Lights*: vol.24, p.324.

He also said (to one of his followers):

> '*O Mufaddal, if our followers were to contemplate the Qur'an, they would not doubt our virtue.* ' [180]

He (a) also said:

> '*Allah has made our regency the axis of the Qur'an and that of all books. The clear verses of the Qur'an revolve around it and through it faith is made plain. The Messenger of Allah (S) ordered that the Qur'an and the family of Muhammad (S) be followed saying in his final sermon: 'I leave amongst you the two momentous things – the greater and the lesser. The greater thing is the book of my Lord and the lesser is the people of my household so remember me through them for you will not stray as long as you adhere to these two.* ' [181]

The Intercession of the Qur'an

The Messenger of Allah (S) said:

> '*Intercessors are five in number: the Qur'an, the bond of kinship, trustworthiness, your Prophet, and the people of the household of your Prophet.* ' [182]

Al-Imam al-Saadiq (a) said:

> '*The Qur'an warns those who seek to reach their Lord through their desire for what He has with Him. The Qur'an is an intercessor whose intercession will be accepted.* ' [183]

---

[179] *Seas of Lights*: vol.89, p.27.
[180] *Seas of Lights*: vol.53, p.26.
[181] *Seas of Lights*: vol.89, p.27.
[182] *Seas of Lights*: vol.8, p.43.
[183] *Seas of Lights*: vol.7, p.12.

The Qur'an as a Cure

The Messenger of Allah (S) said:

> 'He who seeks a cure in other than the Qur'an will never find a cure.' [184]

He (S) also said:

> 'Honey is a cure for every illness and the Qur'an is a cure for what is in the heart so take the two cures – honey and the Qur'an.' [185]

He (S) said:

> 'The Qur'an is the cure.' [186]

Amir al-Mu'minin 'Ali (a) said:

> 'In the Qur'an there is a verse which contains the complete medicine: {**Eat and drink but not to excess.**} [187] [188]

Al-Imam al-Saadiq (a) said:

> 'The cure is in the knowledge of the Qur'an.' [189]

And he (a) also said:

> 'Treat your diseases through charity and seek a cure with the Qur'an for whoever the Qur'an cannot cure there is no cure for him.' [190]

Imam al-Kaadhem (a) said:

> 'In the Qur'an there is a cure for every illness.' [191]

* * *

---

[184] *Appendix to the Shi'a Guide to the Shari'a*: vol.4, p.312.
[185] *Seas of Lights*: vol.63, p.295.
[186] *Seas of Lights*: vol.89, p.176.
[187] *The Qur'an*: The Heights (7):31.
[188] *Seas of Lights*: vol.59, p.267.
[189] *Seas of Lights*: vol.89, p.102.
[190] *Seas of Lights*: vol.59, p.262.
[191] *Seas of Lights*: vol.59, p.262.

The Author

Ayatollah al-Udhma Imam Muhammad Shirazi is the Religious Authority, or Marje', to millions of Muslims around the globe. A charismatic leader who is known for his high moral values, modesty and spirituality, Imam Shirazi is a mentor and a source of aspiration to Muslims; and the means of access to authentic knowledge and teachings of Islam. He has tirelessly devoted himself, and his life, to the affairs of Muslims in particular, and to that of mankind in general. He has made extensive contributions in various fields of learning ranging from Jurisprudence and Theology to Politics, Economics, Law, Sociology and Human Rights.

Muhammad Shirazi was born in the holy city of Najaf, Iraq, in 1347 AH (Muslim calendar), 1927 AD. He settled in the holy city of Karbala, Iraq, at the age of nine, alongside his father. After primary education, the young Shirazi continued his studies in different branches of learning under his father's guidance as well as those of various other eminent scholars and specialists. In the course of his training he showed a remarkable talent and appetite for learning as well as a tireless commitment to his work and the cause he believed in. His extraordinary ability, and effort, earned him the recognition, by his father and other *Marje's* and scholars, of being a *Mujtahid*; a qualified religious scholar in the sciences of Islamic jurisprudence and law. He was subsequently able to assume the office of the Marje' at the early age of 33 in 1960. His followers are found in many countries around the globe.

Imam Shirazi is distinguished for his intellectual ability and holistic vision. He has written various specialized studies that are considered to be among the most important references in the Islamic sciences of beliefs or doctrine, ethics, politics, economics, sociology, law, human rights, etc. He has enriched the world with his staggering contribution of more than 1000 books, treatise and studies on various branches of learning. His works range from simple introductory books for the young generations to literary and scientific masterpieces. Deeply rooted in the holy Qur'an and the Teachings of the Prophet of Islam, his vision and theories cover areas such as Politics, Economics, Government, Management, Sociology, Theology, Philosophy, History and Islamic Law. His work on Islamic Jurisprudence (al-Fiqh series) for example constitutes 150 volumes, which run into more than 70,000 pages. Through his original thoughts and ideas he has championed the causes of issues such as the family, human right, freedom of expression, political pluralism, non-violence, and Shura or consultative system of leadership.

Imam Shirazi believes in the fundamental and elementary nature of freedom in mankind. He calls for freedom of expression, political plurality, debate and discussion, tolerance and forgiveness. He strongly believes in the consultative system of leadership and calls for the establishment of the leadership council of religious authorities. He calls for the establishment of the universal Islamic government to encompass all the Muslim countries. These and other ideas are discussed in detail in his books.

o-o-o-o-O-o-o-o-o

Teachings of Islam

www.shirazi.org.uk

A site dedicated to the cause of Islam, Muslims and Mankind.

Islam aims to bring about prosperity to all mankind. One of the leading authorities on Islam today, Imam Muhammad Shirazi, calls upon all Muslims to adhere to the teachings of Islam in all domains in order to regain their former glory and the salvation of mankind. These teachings include:

- PEACE in every aspect.
- NON-VIOLENCE in all conducts.
- FREEDOM of expression, belief, etc.
- PLURALISM of political parties.
- CONSULTATIVE System of Leadership.
- The re-creation of the single Muslim nation - without geographical borders, passports between them, as stated by Allah:

  "This, your community is a single community and I am your Lord; so worship Me."

- The revival of Islamic brotherhood throughout this nation:

  "The believers are brothers."

- Freedom from all the man-made laws, shackles and restrictions as stated in the Qur'an:

  "... and (the Prophet Muhammad pbuh) releases them from their heavy burdens and from the shackles that were upon them."

This is the official website of Imam Shirazi. You can email your queries on issues of concern to the site at: **queries@shirazi.org.uk**

Other Titles by *fountain books*

www.fountainbooks.co.uk

1. *Aspects of the Political Theory of Imam Muhammad Shirazi*

Muhammad Ayyub is a well-known Islamist political activist within the Iraqi circle who has established a long history of political struggle behind him. He was attracted by the views of the Imam Muhammad Shirazi in the fields of social and political sciences. This prompted the author to write this book to introduce the reader to these views that have remained relatively unknown to the Muslim activists and reformists. It covers such aspects on politics as freedom of expression, party-political pluralism and organisation, social justice, peace and non-violence, human rights, consultation system of government, etc.

2. *Islamic System of Government*

In this introductory book the author outlines the basic principles of a government based on the teachings of Islam. The author begins with the aim and objectives of the government according to Islam and the extent of its authority. He then addresses, from the Islamic viewpoint, the significance and fundamental nature of such issues as consultative system of government, judicial system, freedoms, party political pluralism, social justice, human rights, foreign policy, etc. The author also outlines the policies of a government on issues such as education, welfare, health, crime, services, etc. as well as such matters as the government's income.

3. *If Islam Were To Be Established*

This book can serve as the Muslim's guide to the Islamic government. If an Islamist opposition group has a plan for an Islamic government, this book would help to check various aspects of the plan. In the absence of such a plan, this book would present one. To the non-Muslims, the book presents a glimpse of a typical Islamic system of government. The book would also serve as a yardstick for anyone to check the practices of any government that claims to have implemented an Islamic system of government.

4. The Family

In this book the author highlights the problems he sees primarily in Islamic societies and particularly in the west today, from the phenomenon of unmarried young men and women through to birth control and contraception. He surveys the idea of marriage in various religions and schools of thought and discusses polygamy from the Islamic perspective. As well as being a call to the Muslim world to revert to the true teachings of Islam, this book can also be of use as an introduction to others who seek some answers to the social problems of today. This is because Islam has detailed teachings, which promise success in every area of human life on individual and societal levels, and what's more their practicality has been historically proven.

5. Fundamentals of Islam

In this book the author outlines the five fundamental principles of Islam, namely the Indivisible Oneness of God *(Tawheed)*, Divine Justice *(Adl)*, Prophethood *(Nubowwah)*, Leadership of mankind *(Imamah)*, and Resurrection *(Me'ad)*. For each principle, the author presents a concise discussion on the significance of the issue concerned.   The book could serve as a good introduction to fundamental Islamic beliefs, both for the Muslim and non-Muslim alike.

6. War, Peace and Non-violence: An Islamic perspective

In this work the author addresses three controversial issues, which have come to be associated with Islam.   Through his extensive knowledge of the teachings of Islam, the author presents the Islamic stand on war, peace and non-violence, as found in the traditions and teachings of the Prophet of Islam, which could serve as exemplary models for Mankind. Detailed accounts of the traditions of Prophet in his dealings with his foes during war or times of peace are presented in this book, which gives the reader a clear insight into the way and the basis upon which the Prophet of Islam used to conduct his affairs in this respect.

Also available from:
- www.amazon.co.uk
- *Alif International,*
  109 Kings Avenue, Watford, Herts. WD1 7SB, UK.
  Telephone: + 44 1923 240 844, Fax: +44 1923 237 722